Georgia O'Keeffe

2016 ENGAGEMENT CALENDAR

PORTLAND, OREGON

Item No. Y206

Pomegranate Communications, Inc.
19018 NE Portal Way, Portland OR 97230

Available in the UK and mainland Europe from Pomegranate Europe Ltd.
Unit 1, Heathcote Business Centre, Hurlbutt Road, Warwick, Warwickshire CV34 6TD, UK

Paintings by Georgia O'Keeffe are published with the permission of the
Georgia O'Keeffe Museum insofar as such permission is required.
Rights owned by the Georgia O'Keeffe Museum are reserved by the Museum.
© 2015 Georgia O'Keeffe Museum / Artists Rights Society (ARS), New York

Pomegranate publishes a wide variety of wall, mini wall, and desk calendars. Our extensive
line of paper gift products and books can be found at retail stores worldwide and online.
For more information or to place an order, please contact
Pomegranate Communications, Inc., 800 227 1428, www.pomegranate.com.

Georgia O'Keeffe (American, 1887–1986)
Flower Abstraction, 1924
Oil on canvas, 122.2 x 76.2 cm (48⅛ x 30 in.)
Whitney Museum of American Art, New York
50th Anniversary Gift of Sandra Payson, 85.47
© 2015 Georgia O'Keeffe Museum / Artists Rights Society (ARS), New York

Designed by Tristen Jackman

Dates in color indicate US federal holidays.
Dates listed for all astronomical events in this calendar are based on Coordinated Universal Time (UTC),
the worldwide system of civil timekeeping. UTC is essentially equivalent to Greenwich Mean Time.
Moon phases and American, Canadian, and UK holidays are noted.
Jewish and Islamic holidays begin at sunset on the day preceding the date listed.
Dates of Islamic holidays are given for North America and are subject to adjustment.

 NEW MOON   FIRST QUARTER   FULL MOON   LAST QUARTER

American artist Georgia O'Keeffe (1887–1986) created a body of work that was uniquely her own. Her subject matter was familiar—flowers, landscapes, buildings—but as she shuttled between objective art and abstraction, O'Keeffe found a way of painting that enabled her to transform the objects and sights that transfixed her. Irises and poppies took on an unprecedented range and intensity of feeling.

O'Keeffe first came to the public's attention during the 1920s and 1930s through her enormous, unique flower paintings and the series of portraits of her taken by photographer and art collector Alfred Stieglitz, whom she married in 1924. In 1929 she traveled to the Southwest and was so impressed by the light, colors, and expanse of the desert landscape that she eventually moved to New Mexico, where she devoted her creative energies to capturing the simple forms and spiritual essence of the land.

O'Keeffe constantly experimented with abstraction and color to create an original, compelling, and powerful style. As she stated, "I think I'd rather let the painting work for itself than help it with the word." The twenty images reproduced in this calendar attest to the talent and vision of one of America's most treasured artists.

2016

JANUARY

s	m	t	w	t	f	s
					1	2
3	4	5	6	7	8	9
10	11	12	13	14	15	16
17	18	19	20	21	22	23
24	25	26	27	28	29	30
31						

FEBRUARY

s	m	t	w	t	f	s
	1	2	3	4	5	6
7	8	9	10	11	12	13
14	15	16	17	18	19	20
21	22	23	24	25	26	27
28	29					

MARCH

s	m	t	w	t	f	s
		1	2	3	4	5
6	7	8	9	10	11	12
13	14	15	16	17	18	19
20	21	22	23	24	25	26
27	28	29	30	31		

APRIL

s	m	t	w	t	f	s
					1	2
3	4	5	6	7	8	9
10	11	12	13	14	15	16
17	18	19	20	21	22	23
24	25	26	27	28	29	30

MAY

s	m	t	w	t	f	s
1	2	3	4	5	6	7
8	9	10	11	12	13	14
15	16	17	18	19	20	21
22	23	24	25	26	27	28
29	30	31				

JUNE

s	m	t	w	t	f	s
			1	2	3	4
5	6	7	8	9	10	11
12	13	14	15	16	17	18
19	20	21	22	23	24	25
26	27	28	29	30		

2016

JULY

s	m	t	w	t	f	s
					1	2
3	4	5	6	7	8	9
10	11	12	13	14	15	16
17	18	19	20	21	22	23
24	25	26	27	28	29	30
31						

AUGUST

s	m	t	w	t	f	s
	1	2	3	4	5	6
7	8	9	10	11	12	13
14	15	16	17	18	19	20
21	22	23	24	25	26	27
28	29	30	31			

SEPTEMBER

s	m	t	w	t	f	s
				1	2	3
4	5	6	7	8	9	10
11	12	13	14	15	16	17
18	19	20	21	22	23	24
25	26	27	28	29	30	

OCTOBER

s	m	t	w	t	f	s
						1
2	3	4	5	6	7	8
9	10	11	12	13	14	15
16	17	18	19	20	21	22
23	24	25	26	27	28	29
30	31					

NOVEMBER

s	m	t	w	t	f	s
		1	2	3	4	5
6	7	8	9	10	11	12
13	14	15	16	17	18	19
20	21	22	23	24	25	26
27	28	29	30			

DECEMBER

s	m	t	w	t	f	s
				1	2	3
4	5	6	7	8	9	10
11	12	13	14	15	16	17
18	19	20	21	22	23	24
25	26	27	28	29	30	31

Georgia O'Keeffe (American, 1887–1986)
White Pansy, 1927
Oil on canvas, 91.7 x 76.3 cm (36⅛ x 30 1/16 in.)
The Cleveland Museum of Art
Bequest of Georgia O'Keeffe, 1987.139
© The Cleveland Museum of Art

January

SUNDAY	MONDAY	TUESDAY	WEDNESDAY	THURSDAY	FRIDAY	SATURDAY
					1	2 ☽
3	4	5	6	7	8	9
10 ●	11	12	13	14	15	16 ◑
17	18	19	20	21	22	23
24 ○	25	26	27	28	29	30
31						

JAN 1   NEW YEAR'S DAY

JAN 4   BANK HOLIDAY (SCOTLAND)

JAN 18   MARTIN LUTHER KING JR. DAY

Dec ❀ Jan

monday   BOXING DAY HOLIDAY (CANADA, UK)

362 28

tuesday

363 29

wednesday

364 30

thursday

365 31

friday   NEW YEAR'S DAY

1 1

saturday

2 2 ◑

sunday

3 3

January

BANK HOLIDAY (SCOTLAND)

monday

4 ₄

tuesday

5 ₅

wednesday

6 ₆

thursday

7 ₇

friday

8 ₈

saturday

9 ₉

JANUARY

s	m	t	w	t	f	s
					1	2
3	4	5	6	7	8	9
10	11	12	13	14	15	16
17	18	19	20	21	22	23
24	25	26	27	28	29	30
31						

sunday

● 10 ₁₀

Georgia O'Keeffe (American, 1887–1986)
Poppies, 1950
Oil on canvas, 91.4 x 76.2 cm (36 x 30 in.)
Milwaukee Art Museum
Gift of Mrs. Harry Lynde Bradley, M1977.133
© Georgia O'Keeffe Museum / Artists Rights Society (ARS), New York
Photograph by John R. Glembin

January

Pack - Denmark

~~chargers~~
~~vitamins~~
listerine
hard mints for colleen
H. cream
powder med.
hormones
makeup
~~2 scones~~
~~Pen + paper~~
~~both glasses~~
passport
money
~~zip bags~~
H. cream
~~blue gum~~
Cards
itenerary copenhagen + barcelona
~~theatre book~~

Itinerary CPH + BAK
hormones
~~Powder Med.~~
Passport
money

monday
11

tuesday
12

wednesday
13

thursday
14

friday
15

saturday
◐ 16

sunday
17

JANUARY

s	m	t	w	t	f	s
					1	2
3	4	5	6	7	8	9
10	11	12	13	14	15	16
17	18	19	20	21	22	23
24	25	26	27	28	29	30
31						

January

monday   **MARTIN LUTHER KING JR. DAY**

18   18

tuesday

19   19

wednesday

20   20

thursday

21   21

friday

22   22

saturday

23   23

sunday

24   24   ○

January

monday
25 25

tuesday
26 26

wednesday
27 27

thursday
28 28

friday
29 29

saturday
30 30

JANUARY

s	m	t	w	t	f	s
					1	2
3	4	5	6	7	8	9
10	11	12	13	14	15	16
17	18	19	20	21	22	23
24	25	26	27	28	29	30
31						

sunday
31 31

Georgia O'Keeffe (American, 1887–1986)
Mariposa Lilies and Indian Paintbrush, 1941
Oil on canvas, 25.4 x 35.6 cm (10 x 14 in.)
Georgia O'Keeffe Museum
Gift of The Georgia O'Keeffe Foundation, 2006.05.168
© 2015 Georgia O'Keeffe Museum / Artists Rights Society (ARS), New York

February

SUNDAY	MONDAY	TUESDAY	WEDNESDAY	THURSDAY	FRIDAY	SATURDAY
	1 ◑	2	3	4	5	6
7	8 ●	9	10	11	12	13
14	15 ◑	16	17	18	19	20
21	22 ○	23	24	25	26	27
28	29					

FEB 8 LUNAR NEW YEAR

FEB 9 MARDI GRAS

FEB 10 ASH WEDNESDAY

FEB 14 VALENTINE'S DAY

FEB 15 PRESIDENTS' DAY

FAMILY DAY (CANADA, SOME PROVINCES)

February

monday

32　1　◑

tuesday

33　2　*Copenhagen*

wednesday

34　3

thursday

35　4

friday

36　5

saturday

37　6

sunday

38　7

February

LUNAR NEW YEAR

monday

● 8 _39_

MARDI GRAS

tuesday

9 _40_

ASH WEDNESDAY

wednesday

10 _41_

thursday

11 _42_

friday

12 _43_

saturday

13 _44_

FEBRUARY

s	m	t	w	t	f	s
	1	2	3	4	5	6
7	8	9	10	11	12	13
14	15	16	17	18	19	20
21	22	23	24	25	26	27
28	29					

VALENTINE'S DAY

sunday

14 _45_

Georgia O'Keeffe (American, 1887–1986)
Jack-in-Pulpit - No. 2, 1930
Oil on canvas, 101.6 x 76.2 cm (40 x 30 in.)
National Gallery of Art, Washington
Alfred Stieglitz Collection, Bequest of Georgia O'Keeffe, 1987.58.1
© National Gallery of Art, Washington

February

PRESIDENTS' DAY
FAMILY DAY (CANADA, SOME PROVINCES)

monday

◐ 15 46

tuesday

16 47

wednesday

17 48

thursday

18 49

friday

19 50

saturday

20 51

FEBRUARY

s	m	t	w	t	f	s
	1	2	3	4	5	6
7	8	9	10	11	12	13
14	15	16	17	18	19	20
21	22	23	24	25	26	27
28	29					

sunday

21 52

February

monday
53 22 ○

tuesday
54 23

wednesday
55 24

thursday
56 25

friday
57 26

saturday
58 27

sunday
59 28

March

SUNDAY	MONDAY	TUESDAY	WEDNESDAY	THURSDAY	FRIDAY	SATURDAY
		1 ◑	2	3	4	5
6	7	8	9 ●	10	11	12
13	14	15 ◑	16	17	18	19
20	21	22	23 ○	24	25	26
27	28	29	30	31 ◑		

MAR 1 ST. DAVID'S DAY (WALES)
MAR 6 MOTHERING SUNDAY (UK)
MAR 8 INTERNATIONAL WOMEN'S DAY
MAR 13 DAYLIGHT SAVING TIME BEGINS
MAR 17 ST. PATRICK'S DAY
BANK HOLIDAY (N. IRELAND)
MAR 20 PALM SUNDAY
VERNAL EQUINOX 04:30 UTC

MAR 24 PURIM
MAR 25 GOOD FRIDAY
BANK HOLIDAY (CANADA, UK)
MAR 27 EASTER
SUMMER TIME BEGINS (UK)
MAR 28 EASTER MONDAY (CANADA, UK EXCEPT SCOTLAND)

Feb ❀ Mar

---

monday

60 29

---

tuesday   ST. DAVID'S DAY (WALES)

61 1 ◑

---

wednesday

62 2

---

thursday

63 3

---

friday

64 4

---

saturday

65 5

---

sunday   MOTHERING SUNDAY (UK)

66 6

March

monday

7 ₆₇

INTERNATIONAL WOMEN'S DAY

tuesday

8 ₆₈

wednesday

● 9 ₆₉

thursday

10 ₇₀

friday

11 ₇₁

saturday

12 ₇₂

MARCH

s	m	t	w	t	f	s
		1	2	3	4	5
6	7	8	9	10	11	12
13	14	15	16	17	18	19
20	21	22	23	24	25	26
27	28	29	30	31		

DAYLIGHT SAVING TIME BEGINS

sunday

13 ₇₃

Georgia O'Keeffe (American, 1887–1986)
The Black Iris, 1926
Oil on canvas, 22.9 x 17.8 cm (9 x 7 in.)
Georgia O'Keeffe Museum
Gift of The Burnett Foundation, 2007.01.019
© 2015 Georgia O'Keeffe Museum / Artists Rights Society (ARS), New York

March

monday
14 74

tuesday
◑ ## 15 75

wednesday
16 76

ST. PATRICK'S DAY
BANK HOLIDAY (N. IRELAND)

thursday
17 77

friday
18 78

saturday
19 79

MARCH

s	m	t	w	t	f	s
		1	2	3	4	5
6	7	8	9	10	11	12
13	14	15	16	17	18	19
20	21	22	23	24	25	26
27	28	29	30	31		

PALM SUNDAY
VERNAL EQUINOX 04:30 UTC

sunday
20 80

March

monday

81 21

tuesday

82 22

wednesday

83 23 ○

thursday   PURIM

84 24

friday   GOOD FRIDAY
                                    BANK HOLIDAY (CANADA, UK)

85 25

saturday

86 26

sunday   EASTER
                                     SUMMER TIME BEGINS (UK)

87 27

April

SUNDAY	MONDAY	TUESDAY	WEDNESDAY	THURSDAY	FRIDAY	SATURDAY
				1	2	
3	4	5	6	7 ●	8	9
10	11	12	13	14 ◑	15	16
17	18	19	20	21	22 ○	23
24	25	26	27	28	29	30 ◑

APR 22   EARTH DAY

APR 23   PASSOVER BEGINS
ST. GEORGE'S DAY (ENGLAND)

Georgia O'Keeffe (American, 1887–1986)
White Flower, 1929
Oil on canvas, 76.2 x 91.5 cm (30 x 36 in.)
The Cleveland Museum of Art
Hinman B. Hurlbut Collection, 2162.1930
© 2015 Georgia O'Keeffe Museum / Artists Rights Society (ARS), New York

Mar ✿ Apr

EASTER MONDAY (CANADA, UK EXCEPT SCOTLAND)

monday

28 ₈₈

tuesday

29 ₈₉

wednesday

30 ₉₀

thursday

◑ 31 ₉₁

friday

1 ₉₂

saturday

2 ₉₃

APRIL

s	m	t	w	t	f	s
					1	2
3	4	5	6	7	8	9
10	11	12	13	14	15	16
17	18	19	20	21	22	23
24	25	26	27	28	29	30

sunday

3 ₉₄

April

monday

95 4

tuesday

96 5

wednesday

97 6

thursday

98 7 ●

friday

99 8

saturday

100 9

sunday

101 10

April

monday
11 102

tuesday
12 103

wednesday
13 104

thursday
◐ 14 105

friday
15 106

saturday
16 107

APRIL

s	m	t	w	t	f	s
					1	2
3	4	5	6	7	8	9
10	11	12	13	14	15	16
17	18	19	20	21	22	23
24	25	26	27	28	29	30

sunday
17 108

Georgia O'Keeffe (American, 1887–1986)
Calla Lily Turned Away, 1923
Pastel on cardboard, 35.6 x 27.6 cm (14 x 10⅞ in.)
Georgia O'Keeffe Museum
Gift of The Burnett Foundation, 1997.18.002
© 2015 Georgia O'Keeffe Museum / Artists Rights Society (ARS), New York

April

monday

18 109

tuesday

19 110

wednesday

20 111

thursday

21 112

EARTH DAY

friday

○ 22 113

PASSOVER BEGINS
ST. GEORGE'S DAY (ENGLAND)

saturday

23 114

APRIL

s	m	t	w	t	f	s
					1	2
3	4	5	6	7	8	9
10	11	12	13	14	15	16
17	18	19	20	21	22	23
24	25	26	27	28	29	30

sunday

24 115

Apr ❧ May

monday
25
116

tuesday
26
117

wednesday
27
118

thursday
28
119

friday
29
120

saturday
30 ◑
121

sunday
1
122

May

SUNDAY	MONDAY	TUESDAY	WEDNESDAY	THURSDAY	FRIDAY	SATURDAY
1	2	3	4	5	6 ●	7
8	9	10	11	12	13 ◑	14
15	16	17	18	19	20	21 ○
22	23	24	25	26	27	28
29 ◑	30	31				

MAY 2   BANK HOLIDAY (UK)

MAY 5   CINCO DE MAYO

MAY 8   MOTHER'S DAY

MAY 21   ARMED FORCES DAY

MAY 23   VICTORIA DAY (CANADA)

MAY 30   MEMORIAL DAY

          BANK HOLIDAY (UK)

May

monday   **BANK HOLIDAY (UK)**

123   2

tuesday

124   3

wednesday

125   4

thursday   **CINCO DE MAYO**

126   5

friday

127   6 ●

saturday

128   7

sunday   **MOTHER'S DAY**

129   8

May

monday

9 ₁₃₀

tuesday

10 ₁₃₁

wednesday

11 ₁₃₂

thursday

12 ₁₃₃

friday

◑ 13 ₁₃₄

saturday

14 ₁₃₅

sunday

15 ₁₃₆

MAY

s	m	t	w	t	f	s
1	2	3	4	5	6	7
8	9	10	11	12	13	14
15	16	17	18	19	20	21
22	23	24	25	26	27	28
29	30	31				

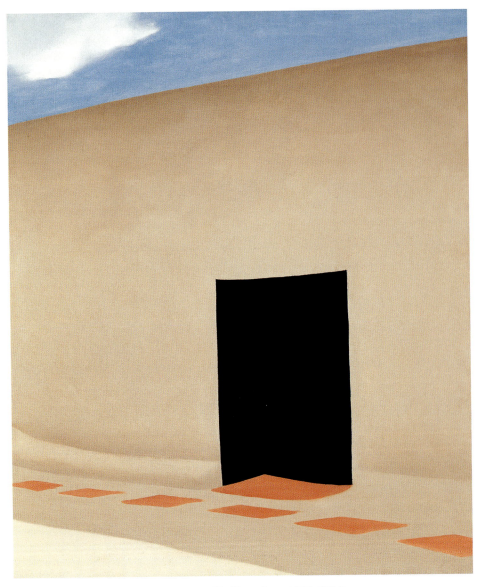

Georgia O'Keeffe (American, 1887–1986)
Patio with Cloud, 1956
Oil on canvas, 91.4 x 76.2 cm (36 x 30 in.)
Milwaukee Art Museum
Gift of Mrs. Edward R. Wehr, M1957.10
© Georgia O'Keeffe Museum / Artists Rights Society (ARS), New York
Photograph by P. Richard Eells

May

monday

16 137

tuesday

17 138

wednesday

18 139

thursday

19 140

friday

20 141

ARMED FORCES DAY

saturday

○ 21 142

MAY

s	m	t	w	t	f	s
1	2	3	4	5	6	7
8	9	10	11	12	13	14
15	16	17	18	19	20	21
22	23	24	25	26	27	28
29	30	31				

sunday

22 143

May

monday
VICTORIA DAY (CANADA)

144 23

tuesday

145 24

wednesday

146 25

thursday

147 26

friday

148 27

saturday

149 28

sunday

150 29 ◗

June

SUNDAY	MONDAY	TUESDAY	WEDNESDAY	THURSDAY	FRIDAY	SATURDAY
			1	2	3	4
5 ●	6	7	8	9	10	11
12 ◐	13	14	15	16	17	18
19	20 ○	21	22	23	24	25
26	27 ◑	28	29	30		

JUN 6	RAMADAN BEGINS	JUN 19	FATHER'S DAY
JUN 14	FLAG DAY	JUN 20	SUMMER SOLSTICE 22:34 UTC

Georgia O'Keeffe (American, 1887–1986)
Sunflower, New Mexico I, 1935
Oil on canvas, 50.8 x 40.6 cm (20 x 16 in.)
The Cleveland Museum of Art
Bequest of Georgia O'Keeffe, 1987.140
© The Cleveland Museum of Art

May ❀ Jun

MEMORIAL DAY
BANK HOLIDAY (UK)

monday
30 151

tuesday
31 152

wednesday
1 153

thursday
2 154

friday
3 155

saturday
4 156

JUNE

s	m	t	w	t	f	s
			1	2	3	4
5	6	7	8	9	10	11
12	13	14	15	16	17	18
19	20	21	22	23	24	25
26	27	28	29	30		

sunday
● 5 157

June

monday   RAMADAN BEGINS

158 6

tuesday

159 7

wednesday

160 8

thursday

161 9

friday

162 10

saturday

163 11

sunday

164 12 ◑

June

monday

13 ₁₆₅

FLAG DAY

tuesday

14 ₁₆₆

wednesday

15 ₁₆₇

thursday

16 ₁₆₈

friday

17 ₁₆₉

saturday

18 ₁₇₀

JUNE

s	m	t	w	t	f	s
			1	2	3	4
5	6	7	8	9	10	11
12	13	14	15	16	17	18
19	20	21	22	23	24	25
26	27	28	29	30		

FATHER'S DAY

sunday

19 ₁₇₁

Georgia O'Keeffe (American, 1887–1986)
White Bird of Paradise, 1939
Oil on canvas, 48.3 x 40.6 cm (19 x 16 in.)
Georgia O'Keeffe Museum
Gift of Jean H. McDonald, (2009.01.001)
© 2015 Georgia O'Keeffe Museum / Artists Rights Society (ARS), New York

June

SUMMER SOLSTICE 22:34 UTC

monday
○ 20 172

tuesday
21 173

wednesday
22 174

thursday
23 175

friday
24 176

saturday
25 177

JUNE

s	m	t	w	t	f	s
			1	2	3	4
5	6	7	8	9	10	11
12	13	14	15	16	17	18
19	20	21	22	23	24	25
26	27	28	29	30		

sunday
26 178

Jun ❀ Jul

monday

179 27 ◑

tuesday

180 28

wednesday

181 29

thursday

182 30

friday   CANADA DAY (CANADA)

183 1

saturday

184 2

sunday

185 3

July

SUNDAY	MONDAY	TUESDAY	WEDNESDAY	THURSDAY	FRIDAY	SATURDAY
					1	2
3	4 ●	5	6	7	8	9
10	11	12 ◐	13	14	15	16
17	18	19 ○	20	21	22	23
24	25	26 ◑	27	28	29	30
31						

JUL 1   CANADA DAY (CANADA)

JUL 4   INDEPENDENCE DAY

JUL 6   EID AL-FITR

JUL 12   BANK HOLIDAY (N. IRELAND)

Georgia O'Keeffe (American, 1887–1986)
Two Pink Shells / Pink Shell, 1937
Oil on canvas, 30.5 x 25.4 cm (12 x 10 in.)
Georgia O'Keeffe Museum
Gift of The Burnett Foundation and The Georgia O'Keeffe Foundation, 1997.04.005
© 2015 Georgia O'Keeffe Museum / Artists Rights Society (ARS), New York

July

INDEPENDENCE DAY

monday

● 4 186

tuesday

5 187

EID AL-FITR

wednesday

6 188

thursday

7 189

friday

8 190

saturday

9 191

JULY

s	m	t	w	t	f	s
					1	2
3	4	5	6	7	8	9
10	11	12	13	14	15	16
17	18	19	20	21	22	23
24	25	26	27	28	29	30
31						

sunday

10 192

July

monday

193 **11**

tuesday   **BANK HOLIDAY (N. IRELAND)**

194 **12** ◐

wednesday

195 **13**

thursday

196 **14**

friday

197 **15**

saturday

198 **16**

sunday

199 **17**

July

monday
18 200

tuesday
○ ### 19 201

wednesday
20 202

thursday
21 203

friday
22 204

saturday
23 205

JULY

s	m	t	w	t	f	s
					1	2
3	4	5	6	7	8	9
10	11	12	13	14	15	16
17	18	19	20	21	22	23
24	25	26	27	28	29	30
31						

sunday
24 206

July

monday

207 25

tuesday

208 26

wednesday

209 27

thursday

210 28

friday

211 29

saturday

212 30

sunday

213 31

August

SUNDAY	MONDAY	TUESDAY	WEDNESDAY	THURSDAY	FRIDAY	SATURDAY
	1	2 ●	3	4	5	6
7	8	9	10 ◐	11	12	13
14	15	16	17	18 ○	19	20
21	22	23	24	25 ◑	26	27
28	29	30	31			

AUG 1   CIVIC HOLIDAY (CANADA, MOST PROVINCES)   AUG 29   BANK HOLIDAY (UK EXCEPT SCOTLAND)
         BANK HOLIDAY (SCOTLAND)

Georgia O'Keeffe (American, 1887–1986)
A Sunflower from Maggie, 1937
Oil on canvas, 40.6 x 50.8 cm (16 x 20 in.)
Museum of Fine Arts, Boston
Alfred Stieglitz Collection—Bequest of Georgia O'Keeffe, 1987.542
© 2007 Museum of Fine Arts, Boston
Photograph © 2015 Museum of Fine Arts, Boston

August

CIVIC HOLIDAY (CANADA, MOST PROVINCES)
BANK HOLIDAY (SCOTLAND)

monday

1 214

tuesday

● 2 215

wednesday

3 216

thursday

4 217

friday

5 218

saturday

6 219

AUGUST

s	m	t	w	t	f	s
	1	2	3	4	5	6
7	8	9	10	11	12	13
14	15	16	17	18	19	20
21	22	23	24	25	26	27
28	29	30	31			

sunday

7 220

August

monday

221 **8**

tuesday

222 **9**

wednesday

223 **10** ◑

thursday

224 **11**

friday

225 **12**

saturday

226 **13**

sunday

227 **14**

August

monday
15 ₂₂₈

tuesday
16 ₂₂₉

wednesday
17 ₂₃₀

thursday
○ ## 18 ₂₃₁

friday
19 ₂₃₂

saturday
20 ₂₃₃

sunday
21 ₂₃₄

AUGUST

s	m	t	w	t	f	s
	1	2	3	4	5	6
7	8	9	10	11	12	13
14	15	16	17	18	19	20
21	22	23	24	25	26	27
28	29	30	31			

Georgia O'Keeffe (American, 1887–1986)
Abstraction White Rose, 1927
Oil on canvas, 91.4 x 76.2 cm (36 x 30 in.)
Georgia O'Keeffe Museum
Gift of The Burnett Foundation and The Georgia O'Keeffe Foundation, 1997.04.002
© 2015 Georgia O'Keeffe Museum / Artists Rights Society (ARS), New York

August

monday
22 235

tuesday
23 236

wednesday
24 237

thursday
◑ 25 238

friday
26 239

saturday
27 240

AUGUST

s	m	t	w	t	f	s
	1	2	3	4	5	6
7	8	9	10	11	12	13
14	15	16	17	18	19	20
21	22	23	24	25	26	27
28	29	30	31			

sunday
28 241

Georgia O'Keeffe (American, 1887–1986)
Apple Family 3, 1921
Oil on canvas, 20.3 x 27.9 cm (8 x 11 in.)
Milwaukee Art Museum
Gift of Jane Bradley Pettit Foundation and The Georgia O'Keeffe Foundation, M1998.82
© Milwaukee Art Museum
Photograph by John R. Glembin

September

SUNDAY	MONDAY	TUESDAY	WEDNESDAY	THURSDAY	FRIDAY	SATURDAY
				1 ●	2	3
4	5	6	7	8	9 ◐	10
11	12	13	14	15	16 ○	17
18	19	20	21	22	23 ◑	24
25	26	27	28	29	30	

SEP   5   LABOR DAY (US, CANADA)
SEP 12   EID AL-ADHA

SEP 21   INTERNATIONAL DAY OF PEACE
SEP 22   AUTUMNAL EQUINOX 14:21 UTC

Aug ❀ Sep

monday   BANK HOLIDAY (UK EXCEPT SCOTLAND)
242 29

tuesday
243 30

wednesday
244 31

thursday
245 1 ●

friday
246 2

saturday
247 3

sunday
248 4

September

LABOR DAY (US, CANADA)

monday

5 249

tuesday

6 250

wednesday

7 251

thursday

8 252

friday

◑ 9 253

saturday

10 254

SEPTEMBER

s	m	t	w	t	f	s
				1	2	3
4	5	6	7	8	9	10
11	12	13	14	15	16	17
18	19	20	21	22	23	24
25	26	27	28	29	30	

sunday

11 255

September

monday   **EID AL-ADHA**

256 **12**

tuesday

257 **13**

wednesday

258 **14**

thursday

259 **15**

friday

260 **16** ○

saturday

261 **17**

sunday

262 **18**

September

monday
19 ₂₆₃

tuesday
20 ₂₆₄

INTERNATIONAL DAY OF PEACE

wednesday
21 ₂₆₅

AUTUMNAL EQUINOX 14:21 UTC

thursday
22 ₂₆₆

friday
23 ₂₆₇

saturday
24 ₂₆₈

SEPTEMBER

s	m	t	w	t	f	s
					1	2	3
4	5	6	7	8	9	10
11	12	13	14	15	16	17
18	19	20	21	22	23	24
25	26	27	28	29	30	

sunday
25 ₂₆₉

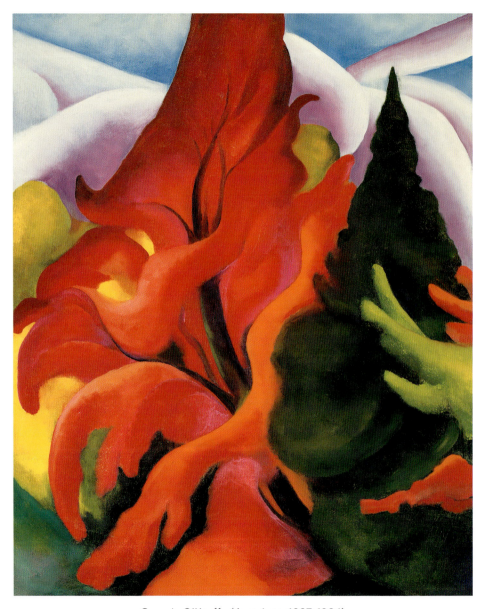

Georgia O'Keeffe (American, 1887–1986)
Trees in Autumn, 1920/1921
Oil on canvas, 64.1 x 51.4 cm (25¼ x 20¼ in.)
Georgia O'Keeffe Museum
Gift of The Burnett Foundation, 1997.06.012
© 2015 Georgia O'Keeffe Museum / Artists Rights Society (ARS), New York

October

SUNDAY	MONDAY	TUESDAY	WEDNESDAY	THURSDAY	FRIDAY	SATURDAY
						1 ●
2	3	4	5	6	7	8
9 ◐	10	11	12	13	14	15
16 ○	17	18	19	20	21	22 ◑
23	24	25	26	27	28	29
30 ●	31					

OCT 2	MUHARRAM		OCT 12	YOM KIPPUR
OCT 3	ROSH HASHANAH		OCT 24	UNITED NATIONS DAY
OCT 10	COLUMBUS DAY		OCT 30	SUMMER TIME ENDS (UK)
	THANKSGIVING DAY (CANADA)		OCT 31	HALLOWEEN
OCT 11	ASHURA			

Sep ❀ Oct

monday
270 **26**

tuesday
271 **27**

wednesday
272 **28**

thursday
273 **29**

friday
274 **30**

saturday
275 **1** ●

sunday   MUHARRAM
276 **2**

October

ROSH HASHANAH

monday

3 277

tuesday

4 278

wednesday

5 279

thursday

6 280

friday

7 281

saturday

8 282

OCTOBER

s	m	t	w	t	f	s
						1
2	3	4	5	6	7	8
9	10	11	12	13	14	15
16	17	18	19	20	21	22
23	24	25	26	27	28	29
30	31					

sunday

9 283

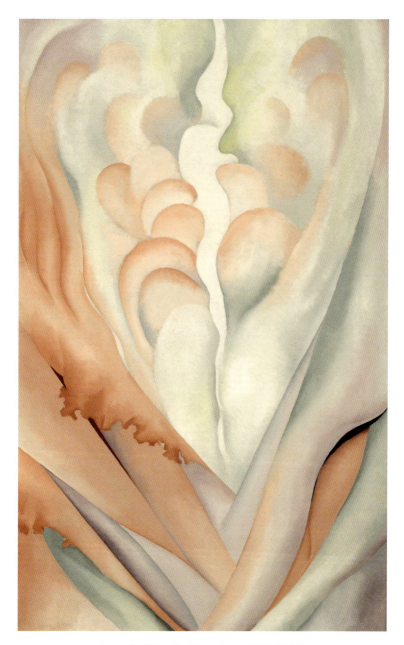

Georgia O'Keeffe (American, 1887–1986)
Flower Abstraction, 1924
Oil on canvas, 122.2 x 76.2 cm (48⅛ x 30 in.)
Whitney Museum of American Art, New York
50th Anniversary Gift of Sandra Payson, 85.47
© 2015 Georgia O'Keeffe Museum / Artists Rights Society (ARS), New York

October

COLUMBUS DAY
THANKSGIVING DAY (CANADA)

monday
10 284

ASHURA

tuesday
11 285

YOM KIPPUR

wednesday
12 286

thursday
13 287

friday
14 288

saturday
15 289

OCTOBER

s	m	t	w	t	f	s
						1
2	3	4	5	6	7	8
9	10	11	12	13	14	15
16	17	18	19	20	21	22
23	24	25	26	27	28	29
30	31					

sunday
○ 16 290

October

monday

291   17

tuesday

292   18

wednesday

293   19

thursday

294   20

friday

295   21

saturday

296   22

sunday

297   23

October

UNITED NATIONS DAY

monday
24 298

tuesday
25 299

wednesday
26 300

thursday
27 301

friday
28 302

saturday
29 303

OCTOBER

s	m	t	w	t	f	s
						1
2	3	4	5	6	7	8
9	10	11	12	13	14	15
16	17	18	19	20	21	22
23	24	25	26	27	28	29
30	31					

SUMMER TIME ENDS (UK)

sunday
● 30 304

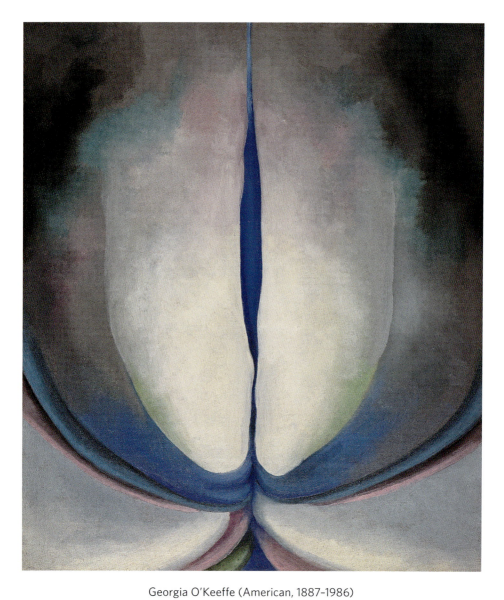

Georgia O'Keeffe (American, 1887–1986)
Blue Line, 1919
Oil on canvas, 51.1 x 43.5 cm (20⅛ x 17⅛ in.)
Georgia O'Keeffe Museum
Gift of The Burnett Foundation and The Georgia O'Keeffe Foundation, 1997.04.004
© 2015 Georgia O'Keeffe Museum / Artists Rights Society (ARS), New York

November

SUNDAY	MONDAY	TUESDAY	WEDNESDAY	THURSDAY	FRIDAY	SATURDAY
		1	2	3	4	5
6	7 ☽	8	9	10	11	12
13	14 ○	15	16	17	18	19
20	21 ◑	22	23	24	25	26
27	28	29 ●	30			

NOV 6   DAYLIGHT SAVING TIME ENDS
NOV 8   ELECTION DAY
NOV 11   VETERANS DAY
         REMEMBRANCE DAY (CANADA)

NOV 24   THANKSGIVING DAY
NOV 30   ST. ANDREW'S DAY (SCOTLAND)

Oct ❀ Nov

monday
31
305
HALLOWEEN

tuesday
1
306

wednesday
2
307

thursday
3
308

friday
4
309

saturday
5
310

sunday
6
311
DAYLIGHT SAVING TIME ENDS

November

monday

7 312

tuesday

ELECTION DAY

8 313

wednesday

9 314

thursday

10 315

friday

VETERANS DAY
REMEMBRANCE DAY (CANADA)

11 316

saturday

12 317

NOVEMBER

s	m	t	w	t	f	s
		1	2	3	4	5
6	7	8	9	10	11	12
13	14	15	16	17	18	19
20	21	22	23	24	25	26
27	28	29	30			

sunday

13 318

Georgia O'Keeffe (American, 1887–1986)
Red Maple, 1922
Oil on canvas, 63.5 x 50.8 cm (25 x 20 in.)
Georgia O'Keeffe Museum
Gift of The Georgia O'Keeffe Foundation, 2006.05.096
© 2015 Georgia O'Keeffe Museum / Artists Rights Society (ARS), New York

November

monday

○ 14 319

tuesday

15 320

wednesday

16 321

thursday

17 322

friday

18 323

saturday

19 324

NOVEMBER

s	m	t	w	t	f	s
		1	2	3	4	5
6	7	8	9	10	11	12
13	14	15	16	17	18	19
20	21	22	23	24	25	26
27	28	29	30			

sunday

20 325

November

monday

326 21 ◑

tuesday

327 22

wednesday

328 23

thursday   THANKSGIVING DAY

329 24

friday

330 25

saturday

331 26

sunday

332 27

December

SUNDAY	MONDAY	TUESDAY	WEDNESDAY	THURSDAY	FRIDAY	SATURDAY
				1	2	3
4	5	6	7 ◑	8	9	10
11	12	13	14 ○	15	16	17
18	19	20	21 ◐	22	23	24
25	26	27	28	29 ●	30	31

DEC 12	MAWLID AN-NABI	DEC 26	CHRISTMAS HOLIDAY
DEC 21	WINTER SOLSTICE 10:44 UTC		BOXING DAY (CANADA, UK)
DEC 25	CHRISTMAS		KWANZAA BEGINS
	HANUKKAH BEGINS	DEC 27	CHRISTMAS HOLIDAY (CANADA, UK)

Georgia O'Keeffe (American, 1887–1986)
Untitled (Purple Petunia), 1925
Oil on canvas, 18.4 x 18.4 cm (7¼ x 7¼ in.)
Georgia O'Keeffe Museum
Gift of The Burnett Foundation, 1997.06.021
© 2015 Georgia O'Keeffe Museum / Artists Rights Society (ARS), New York

Nov ✿ Dec

monday

28 ₃₃₃

tuesday

● 29 ₃₃₄

ST. ANDREW'S DAY (SCOTLAND)   *wednesday*

30 ₃₃₅

thursday

1 ₃₃₆

friday

2 ₃₃₇

saturday

3 ₃₃₈

DECEMBER

s	m	t	w	t	f	s
				1	2	3
4	5	6	7	8	9	10
11	12	13	14	15	16	17
18	19	20	21	22	23	24
25	26	27	28	29	30	31

sunday

4 ₃₃₉

December

monday

340 **5**

tuesday

341 **6**

wednesday

342 **7** ◐

thursday

343 **8**

friday

344 **9**

saturday

345 **10**

sunday

346 **11**

December

MAWLID AN-NABI

monday
12 ₃₄₇

tuesday
13 ₃₄₈

wednesday
○ 14 ₃₄₉

thursday
15 ₃₅₀

friday
16 ₃₅₁

saturday
17 ₃₅₂

DECEMBER

s	m	t	w	t	f	s
				1	2	3
4	5	6	7	8	9	10
11	12	13	14	15	16	17
18	19	20	21	22	23	24
25	26	27	28	29	30	31

sunday
18 ₃₅₃

Georgia O'Keeffe (American, 1887–1986)
The White Calico Flower, 1931
Oil on canvas, 76.7 x 91.9 cm (30³⁄₁₆ x 36³⁄₁₆ in.)
Whitney Museum of American Art, New York
Purchase 32.26
© 2015 Georgia O'Keeffe Museum / Artists Rights Society (ARS), New York

December

monday
19
354

tuesday
20
355

WINTER SOLSTICE 10:44 UTC

wednesday
◑ 21
356

thursday
22
357

friday
23
358

saturday
24
359

DECEMBER

s	m	t	w	t	f	s
				1	2	3
4	5	6	7	8	9	10
11	12	13	14	15	16	17
18	19	20	21	22	23	24
25	26	27	28	29	30	31

CHRISTMAS
HANUKKAH BEGINS

sunday
25
360

Dec ❀ Jan 2017

---

monday
361 **26**

CHRISTMAS HOLIDAY
BOXING DAY (CANADA, UK)
KWANZAA BEGINS

---

tuesday
362 **27**

CHRISTMAS HOLIDAY (CANADA, UK)

---

wednesday
363 **28**

---

thursday
364 **29** ●

---

friday
365 **30**

---

saturday
366 **31**

---

sunday
1 **1**

NEW YEAR'S DAY

January 2017

SUNDAY	MONDAY	TUESDAY	WEDNESDAY	THURSDAY	FRIDAY	SATURDAY
1	2	3	4	5 ◐	6	7
8	9	10	11	12 ○	13	14
15	16	17	18	19 ◑	20	21
22	23	24	25	26	27	28 ●
29	30	31				

JAN 1	NEW YEAR'S DAY	
JAN 2	NEW YEAR'S DAY HOLIDAY	
JAN 3	BANK HOLIDAY (SCOTLAND)	
JAN 16	MARTIN LUTHER KING JR. DAY	
JAN 28	LUNAR NEW YEAR	

January 2017

monday   NEW YEAR'S DAY HOLIDAY

2 2

tuesday   BANK HOLIDAY (SCOTLAND)

3 3

wednesday

4 4

thursday

5 5 ◑

friday

6 6

saturday

7 7

sunday

8 8

January 2017

monday

9 ₉

tuesday

10 ₁₀

wednesday

11 ₁₁

thursday

○ 12 ₁₂

friday

13 ₁₃

saturday

14 ₁₄

JANUARY

s	m	t	w	t	f	s
1	2	3	4	5	6	7
8	9	10	11	12	13	14
15	16	17	18	19	20	21
22	23	24	25	26	27	28
29	30	31				

sunday

15 ₁₅

January 2017

monday   MARTIN LUTHER KING JR. DAY

16   16

tuesday

17   17

wednesday

18   18

thursday

19   19   ◑

friday

20   20

saturday

21   21

sunday

22   22

January 2017

monday
23 ₂₃

tuesday
24 ₂₄

wednesday
25 ₂₅

thursday
26 ₂₆

friday
27 ₂₇

LUNAR NEW YEAR

saturday
● ## 28 ₂₈

JANUARY

s	m	t	w	t	f	s
1	2	3	4	5	6	7
8	9	10	11	12	13	14
15	16	17	18	19	20	21
22	23	24	25	26	27	28
29	30	31				

sunday
29 ₂₉

2017

JANUARY

s	m	t	w	t	f	s
1	2	3	4	5	6	7
8	9	10	11	12	13	14
15	16	17	18	19	20	21
22	23	24	25	26	27	28
29	30	31				

FEBRUARY

s	m	t	w	t	f	s
			1	2	3	4
5	6	7	8	9	10	11
12	13	14	15	16	17	18
19	20	21	22	23	24	25
26	27	28				

MARCH

s	m	t	w	t	f	s
			1	2	3	4
5	6	7	8	9	10	11
12	13	14	15	16	17	18
19	20	21	22	23	24	25
26	27	28	29	30	31	

APRIL

s	m	t	w	t	f	s
						1
2	3	4	5	6	7	8
9	10	11	12	13	14	15
16	17	18	19	20	21	22
23	24	25	26	27	28	29
30						

MAY

s	m	t	w	t	f	s
	1	2	3	4	5	6
7	8	9	10	11	12	13
14	15	16	17	18	19	20
21	22	23	24	25	26	27
28	29	30	31			

JUNE

s	m	t	w	t	f	s
				1	2	3
4	5	6	7	8	9	10
11	12	13	14	15	16	17
18	19	20	21	22	23	24
25	26	27	28	29	30	

2017

JULY

s	m	t	w	t	f	s
						1
2	3	4	5	6	7	8
9	10	11	12	13	14	15
16	17	18	19	20	21	22
23	24	25	26	27	28	29
30	31					

AUGUST

s	m	t	w	t	f	s
		1	2	3	4	5
6	7	8	9	10	11	12
13	14	15	16	17	18	19
20	21	22	23	24	25	26
27	28	29	30	31		

SEPTEMBER

s	m	t	w	t	f	s
					1	2
3	4	5	6	7	8	9
10	11	12	13	14	15	16
17	18	19	20	21	22	23
24	25	26	27	28	29	30

OCTOBER

s	m	t	w	t	f	s
1	2	3	4	5	6	7
8	9	10	11	12	13	14
15	16	17	18	19	20	21
22	23	24	25	26	27	28
29	30	31				

NOVEMBER

s	m	t	w	t	f	s
			1	2	3	4
5	6	7	8	9	10	11
12	13	14	15	16	17	18
19	20	21	22	23	24	25
26	27	28	29	30		

DECEMBER

s	m	t	w	t	f	s
					1	2
3	4	5	6	7	8	9
10	11	12	13	14	15	16
17	18	19	20	21	22	23
24	25	26	27	28	29	30
31						

2017 YEAR PLANNER

	JANUARY		FEBRUARY
1	s	New Year's Day	w
2	m	New Year's Day Holiday	th
3	t	Bank Holiday (Scotland)	f
4	w		s
5	th		s
6	f		m
7	s		t
8	s		w
9	m		th
10	t		f
11	w		s
12	th		s
13	f		m
14	s		t	Valentine's Day
15	s		w
16	m	Martin Luther King Jr. Day	th
17	t		f
18	w		s
19	th		s
20	f		m	**Presidents' Day** Family Day (Canada, some provinces)
21	s		t
22	s		w
23	m		th
24	t		f
25	w		s
26	th		s
27	f		m
28	s	Lunar New Year	t	Mardi Gras
29	s		
30	m		
31	t		

2017 YEAR PLANNER

	MARCH		APRIL
1	w	Ash Wednesday / St. David's Day (Wales)	s
2	th		s
3	f		m
4	s		t
5	s		w
6	m		th
7	t		f
8	w	International Women's Day	s
9	th		s — Palm Sunday
10	f		m
11	s		t — Passover begins
12	s	Purim / Daylight Saving Time begins	w
13	m		th
14	t		f — Good Friday / Bank Holiday (Canada, UK)
15	w		s
16	th		s — Easter
17	f	St. Patrick's Day / Bank Holiday (N. Ireland)	m — Easter Monday (Canada, UK except Scotland)
18	s		t
19	s		w
20	m	Vernal Equinox 10:29 UTC	th
21	t		f
22	w		s
23	th		s — Earth Day
24	f		m — St. George's Day (England)
25	s		t
26	s	Mothering Sunday (UK) / Summer Time begins (UK)	w
27	m		th
28	t		f
29	w		s
30	th		s
31	f		

2017 YEAR PLANNER

	MAY		JUNE
1	m	Bank Holiday (UK)	th
2	t		f
3	w		s
4	th		s
5	f	Cinco de Mayo	m
6	s		t
7	s		w
8	m		th
9	t		f
10	w		s
11	th		s
12	f		m
13	s		t
14	s	Mother's Day	w	Flag Day
15	m		th
16	t		f
17	w		s
18	th		s	Father's Day
19	f		m
20	s	Armed Forces Day	t
21	s		w	Summer Solstice 04:24 UTC
22	m	Victoria Day (Canada)	th
23	t		f
24	w		s
25	th		s	Eid al-Fitr
26	f		m
27	s	Ramadan begins	t
28	s		w
29	m	**Memorial Day** Bank Holiday (UK)	th
30	t		f
31	w		

2017 YEAR PLANNER

	JULY		AUGUST
1	s	Canada Day (Canada)	t	
2	s		w	
3	m	Canada Day Holiday (Canada)	th	
4	t	**Independence Day**	f	
5	w		s	
6	th		s	
7	f		m	Civic Holiday (Canada, most provinces) / Bank Holiday (Scotland)
8	s		t	
9	s		w	
10	m		th	
11	t		f	
12	w	Bank Holiday (N. Ireland)	s	
13	th		s	
14	f		m	
15	s		t	
16	s		w	
17	m		th	
18	t		f	
19	w		s	
20	th		s	
21	f		m	
22	s		t	
23	s		w	
24	m		th	
25	t		f	
26	w		s	
27	th		s	
28	f		m	Bank Holiday (UK except Scotland)
29	s		t	
30	s		w	
31	m		th	

2017 YEAR PLANNER

	SEPTEMBER		OCTOBER
1	f	Eid al-Adha	s	
2	s		m	
3	s		t	
4	m	**Labor Day** (US, Canada)	w	
5	t		th	
6	w		f	
7	th		s	
8	f		s	
9	s		m	**Columbus Day** Thanksgiving Day (Canada)
10	s		t	
11	m		w	
12	t		th	
13	w		f	
14	th		s	
15	f		s	
16	s		m	
17	s		t	
18	m		w	
19	t		th	
20	w		f	
21	th	Rosh Hashanah International Day of Peace • Muharram	s	
22	f	Autumnal Equinox 20:02 UTC	s	
23	s		m	
24	s		t	United Nations Day
25	m		w	
26	t		th	
27	w		f	
28	th		s	
29	f		s	Summer Time ends (UK)
30	s	Yom Kippur Ashura	m	
31			t	Halloween

2017 YEAR PLANNER

	NOVEMBER		DECEMBER
1	w	f	Mawlid an-Nabi
2	th	s	
3	f	s	
4	s	m	
5	s	Daylight Saving Time ends	t	
6	m	w	
7	t	th	
8	w	f	
9	th	s	
10	f	**Veterans Day Holiday**	s	
11	s	**Veterans Day** Remembrance Day (Canada)	m	
12	s	t	
13	m	Remembrance Day Holiday (Canada)	w	Hanukkah begins
14	t	th	
15	w	f	
16	th	s	
17	f	s	
18	s	m	
19	s	t	
20	m	w	
21	t	th	Winter Solstice 16:28 UTC
22	w	f	
23	th	**Thanksgiving Day**	s	
24	f	s	
25	s	m	**Christmas**
26	s	t	Boxing Day (Canada, UK) Kwanzaa begins
27	m	w	
28	t	th	
29	w	f	
30	th	St. Andrew's Day (Scotland)	s	
31		s	

January

Notes & Expenses

Notes & Expenses

February

March

Notes & Expenses

Notes & Expenses   April

May   Notes & Expenses

Notes & Expenses

June

July

Notes & Expenses

Notes & Expenses   August

September   Notes & Expenses

Notes & Expenses   October

November   Notes & Expenses

Notes & Expenses

December

2016 INTERNATIONAL HOLIDAYS

Following are the dates of major holidays and religious observances in 2016 for selected countries. Those of the United States, the United Kingdom, and Canada appear on this calendar's grid pages. Jewish and Islamic observances begin at sunset on the day preceding the date listed. Some dates are subject to government adjustment; all should be confirmed with local sources before making international travel or business plans. Pomegranate is not responsible for any errors or omissions in this list.

ARGENTINA
1	Jan	New Year's Day
8-9	Feb	Carnival
24	Mar	Truth and Justice Day
		Maundy Thursday
25	Mar	Good Friday
27	Mar	Easter
2	Apr	Malvinas Day
1	May	Labor Day
25	May	First Government Day
20	Jun	Belgrano Day
8	Jul	Public Holiday
9	Jul	Independence Day
15	Aug	San Martín Day
10	Oct	Cultural Diversity Day
28	Nov	National Sovereignty Day
8	Dec	Immaculate Conception
9	Dec	Public Holiday
24	Dec	Christmas Eve (afternoon)
25	Dec	Christmas
31	Dec	New Year's Eve (afternoon)

AUSTRALIA
1	Jan	New Year's Day
26	Jan	Australia Day
7	Mar	Labor Day (WA)
14	Mar	Adelaide Cup Day (SA)
		Canberra Day (ACT)
		Eight Hours Day (TAS)
		Labor Day (VIC)
25-28	Mar	Easter Holiday
29	Mar	Easter Tuesday (TAS)
25	Apr	Anzac Day
2	May	Labor Day / May Day (NT)
6	Jun	Western Australia Day (WA)
13	Jun	Queen's Birthday (except WA)
1	Aug	Picnic Day (NT)
		Bank Holiday (NSW)
26	Sep	Queen's Birthday (WA)
3	Oct	Labor Day (ACT, NSW, QLD, SA)
10	Oct	Family and Community Day (ACT)
1	Nov	Melbourne Cup Day (VIC)
25	Dec	Christmas
26	Dec	Boxing Day / Proclamation Day
27	Dec	Christmas Holiday

BRAZIL
1	Jan	New Year's Day
8-9	Feb	Carnival
10	Feb	Ash Wednesday (until 2 p.m.)
25	Mar	Good Friday
27	Mar	Easter
21	Apr	Tiradentes Day
1	May	Labor Day
26	May	Corpus Christi
7	Sep	Independence Day
12	Oct	Our Lady of Aparecida
28	Oct	Civil Servants' Day
2	Nov	All Souls' Day
15	Nov	Republic Day
20	Nov	Black Consciousness Day
24	Dec	Christmas Eve (after 2 p.m.)
25	Dec	Christmas
31	Dec	New Year's Eve (after 2 p.m.)

CHINA (SEE ALSO HONG KONG)
1	Jan	New Year's Day
8-14	Feb	Spring Festival
4	Apr	Tomb-Sweeping Day
1-2	May	Labor Day Holiday
9-10	Jun	Dragon Boat Festival Holiday
15-16	Sep	Mid-Autumn Festival Holiday
1-7	Oct	National Day Holiday

FRANCE
1	Jan	New Year's Day
27	Mar	Easter
28	Mar	Easter Monday
1	May	Labor Day
5	May	Ascension Day
8	May	Victory Day
16	May	Whit Monday
14	Jul	National Day
15	Aug	Assumption
1	Nov	All Saints' Day
11	Nov	Armistice Day
25	Dec	Christmas

GERMANY
1	Jan	New Year's Day
25	Mar	Good Friday
27	Mar	Easter
28	Mar	Easter Monday
1	May	Labor Day
5	May	Ascension Day
16	May	Whit Monday
3	Oct	Unity Day
25-26	Dec	Christmas Holiday

HONG KONG
1	Jan	New Year's Day
8-10	Feb	Lunar New Year Holiday
25	Mar	Good Friday
26	Mar	Holy Saturday
27	Mar	Easter
28	Mar	Easter Monday
4	Apr	Tomb-Sweeping Day
1-2	May	Labor Day Holiday
14	May	Buddha's Birthday
9	Jun	Dragon Boat Festival
1	Jul	Special Administrative Region Establishment Day
16	Sep	Day after Mid-Autumn Festival
1	Oct	National Day
9-10	Oct	Chung Yeung Festival Holiday
25-27	Dec	Christmas Holiday

INDIA
1	Jan	New Year's Day
14	Jan	Makar Sankranti
26	Jan	Republic Day
7	Mar	Maha Shivaratri
23	Mar	Holi
25	Mar	Good Friday
27	Mar	Easter
1	Apr	Bank Holiday
14	Apr	Dr. B. R. Ambedkar's Birthday
15	Apr	Ram Navami
19	Apr	Mahavir Jayanti
1	May	May Day
21	May	Buddha Purnima
6	Jul	Ramzan Eid (Eid al-Fitr)
15	Aug	Independence Day
25	Aug	Janmashtami
12	Sep	Bakr Eid (Eid al-Adha)
30	Sep	Bank Holiday
2	Oct	Mahatma Gandhi's Birthday
11	Oct	Dussehra (Vijaya Dashami)
12	Oct	Muharram
30	Oct	Diwali (Deepavali)
14	Nov	Guru Nanak's Birthday
12	Dec	Milad un-Nabi
25	Dec	Christmas

IRELAND
1	Jan	New Year's Day
17	Mar	St. Patrick's Day
25	Mar	Bank Holiday
27	Mar	Easter
28	Mar	Easter Monday
2	May	Bank Holiday
6	Jun	Bank Holiday
1	Aug	Bank Holiday
31	Oct	Bank Holiday
25	Dec	Christmas
26	Dec	St. Stephen's Day
27-28	Dec	Bank Holiday

ISRAEL
24	Mar	Purim (except Jerusalem)
25	Mar	Shushan Purim (Jerusalem)
23	Apr	First day of Pesach (Passover)
29	Apr	Last day of Pesach (Passover)
11	May	Bank Holiday (afternoon)
12	May	Independence Day Holiday
12	Jun	Shavuot
3-4	Oct	Rosh Hashanah Holiday
12	Oct	Yom Kippur
16	Oct	Bank Holiday (afternoon)
17	Oct	First day of Sukkot
24	Oct	Shemini Atzeret / Simhat Torah

ITALY
1	Jan	New Year's Day
6	Jan	Epiphany
27	Mar	Easter
28	Mar	Easter Monday
25	Apr	Liberation Day
1	May	Labor Day
2	Jun	National Day
29	Jun	Sts. Peter and Paul (Rome)
15	Aug	Assumption
1	Nov	All Saints' Day
8	Dec	Immaculate Conception
25	Dec	Christmas
26	Dec	St. Stephen's Day

Japan

1	Jan	New Year's Day
11	Jan	Coming of Age Day
11	Feb	Foundation Day
20-21	Mar	Vernal Equinox Holiday
29	Apr	Shōwa Day
3	May	Constitution Day
4	May	Greenery Day
5	May	Children's Day
18	Jul	Marine Day
19	Sep	Respect for the Aged Day
22	Sep	Autumnal Equinox
10	Oct	Fitness Day
3	Nov	Culture Day
23	Nov	Labor Thanksgiving Day
23	Dec	Emperor's Birthday
29-30	Dec	New Year's Holiday

Mexico

1	Jan	New Year's Day
1	Feb	Constitution Day Holiday
21	Mar	Benito Juárez's Birthday
24	Mar	Maundy Thursday
25	Mar	Good Friday
27	Mar	Easter
1	May	Labor Day
16	Sep	Independence Day
2	Nov	All Souls' Day (Day of the Dead)
21	Nov	Revolution Day Holiday
12	Dec	Our Lady of Guadalupe
25	Dec	Christmas

Netherlands

1	Jan	New Year's Day
25	Mar	Good Friday
27	Mar	Easter
28	Mar	Easter Monday
27	Apr	King's Day
5	May	Ascension Day Liberation Day
15	May	Pentecost
16	May	Whit Monday
25-26	Dec	Christmas Holiday

New Zealand

1-2, 4	Jan	New Year's Holiday
25	Jan	Wellington Anniversary Day
1	Feb	Auckland Anniversary Day Nelson Anniversary Day
6	Feb	Waitangi Day
8	Feb	Waitangi Day Holiday
21	Mar	Otago Anniversary Day
25	Mar	Good Friday
27	Mar	Easter
28	Mar	Easter Monday
25	Apr	Anzac Day
6	Jun	Queen's Birthday
24	Oct	Labor Day
11	Nov	Canterbury Anniversary Day
25	Dec	Christmas
26	Dec	Boxing Day
27	Dec	Christmas Holiday

Puerto Rico

All US federal holidays are observed, in addition to the following:

6	Jan	Epiphany
11	Jan	Eugenio María de Hostos Day
22	Mar	Emancipation Day
25	Mar	Good Friday
27	Mar	Easter
18	Apr	José de Diego Day
18	Jul	Luis Muñoz Rivera Day
25	Jul	Constitution Day
27	Jul	José Celso Barbosa Day
19	Nov	Puerto Rico Discovery Day
24	Dec	Christmas Eve (afternoon)

Russia

1-8	Jan	New Year's and Orthodox Christmas Holiday
23	Feb	Motherland Defender's Day
8	Mar	International Women's Day
1-2	May	Labor Day Holiday
9	May	Victory Day
12-13	Jun	Russia Day Holiday
4	Nov	Unity Day

Singapore

1	Jan	New Year's Day
8-9	Feb	Chinese New Year Holiday
25	Mar	Good Friday
27	Mar	Easter
1-2	May	Labor Day Holiday
21	May	Vesak Day (Buddha Day)
6	Jul	Hari Raya Puasa (Eid al-Fitr)
9	Aug	National Day
12	Sep	Hari Raya Haji (Eid al-Adha)
29	Oct	Deepavali
25-26	Dec	Christmas Holiday

South Africa

1	Jan	New Year's Day
21	Mar	Human Rights Day
25	Mar	Good Friday
27	Mar	Easter
28	Mar	Family Day / Easter Monday
27	Apr	Freedom Day
1	May	Workers' Day
2	May	Public Holiday
16	Jun	Youth Day
9	Aug	National Women's Day
24	Sep	Heritage Day
16	Dec	Reconciliation Day
25	Dec	Christmas
26	Dec	Day of Goodwill

South Korea

1	Jan	New Year's Day
7-10	Feb	Lunar New Year Holiday
1	Mar	Samil Day
1	May	Labor Day
5	May	Children's Day
14	May	Buddha Day
6	Jun	Memorial Day
15	Aug	Independence Day
14-16	Sep	Harvest Moon Festival
3	Oct	Foundation Day
9	Oct	Hangeul Day
25	Dec	Christmas

Spain

1	Jan	New Year's Day
6	Jan	Epiphany
24	Mar	Maundy Thursday
25	Mar	Good Friday
27	Mar	Easter
1	May	Labor Day
15	Aug	Assumption
12	Oct	National Day
1	Nov	All Saints' Day
6	Dec	Constitution Day
8	Dec	Immaculate Conception
25	Dec	Christmas

Sweden

1	Jan	New Year's Day
5	Jan	Epiphany Eve (afternoon)
6	Jan	Epiphany
24	Mar	Bank Holiday (afternoon)
25	Mar	Good Friday
27	Mar	Easter
28	Mar	Easter Monday
1	May	May Day
5	May	Ascension Day
15	May	Whit Sunday
6	Jun	National Day
24	Jun	Midsummer's Eve
25	Jun	Midsummer's Day
4	Nov	All Hallows' Eve (afternoon)
5	Nov	All Saints' Day
24	Dec	Christmas Eve
25-26	Dec	Christmas Holiday
31	Dec	New Year's Eve

Switzerland

1	Jan	New Year's Day
25	Mar	Good Friday
27	Mar	Easter
28	Mar	Easter Monday
5	May	Ascension Day
16	May	Whit Monday
1	Aug	National Day
25	Dec	Christmas
26	Dec	St. Stephen's Day

Thailand

1	Jan	New Year's Day
23	Feb	Makha Bucha Day
6	Apr	Chakri Day
13-15	Apr	Songkran Holiday
1-2	May	Labor Day Holiday
5	May	Coronation Day
21	May	Visakha Bucha Day (Buddha Day)
23	May	Visakha Bucha Day (Buddha Day) Holiday
1	Jul	Bank Holiday
31	Jul	Asarnha Bucha Day
12	Aug	Queen's Birthday
23-24	Oct	Chulalongkorn Day Holiday
5	Dec	King's Birthday
10	Dec	Constitution Day
12	Dec	Constitution Day Holiday
31	Dec	New Year's Eve

Data supplied by Q++ Studio; for updates and more information, visit www.qppstudio.net.

© 2015 Pomegranate Communications, Inc.

WORLD TIME ZONE MAP

This map is based on Coordinated Universal Time (UTC), the worldwide system of civil timekeeping. UTC is essentially equivalent to Greenwich Mean Time. Zone boundaries are approximate and subject to change. Time differences relative to UTC shown here are based on the use of standard time; where Daylight Saving Time (Summer Time) is employed, add one hour to local standard time.

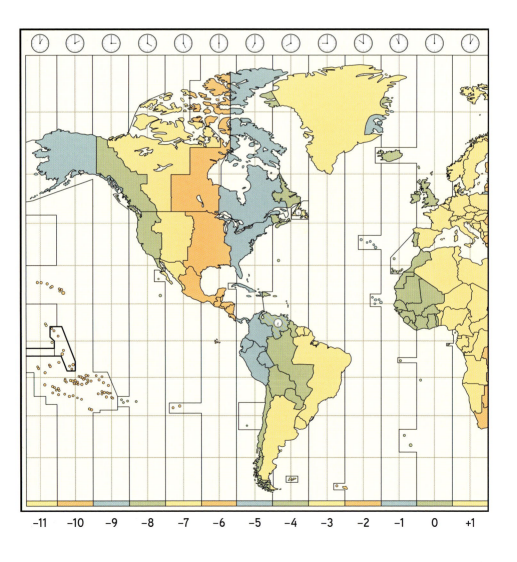

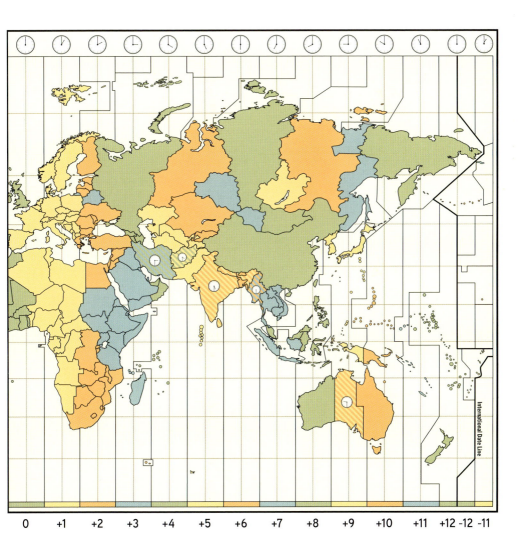

Personal Information

name _____

address _____

city _____ state _____ zip _____

phone _____

mobile _____ fax _____

e-mail _____

in case of emergency, please notify:

name _____

address _____

city _____ state _____ zip _____

phone _____

physician's name _____

physician's phone _____

health insurance company _____

plan number _____

allergies _____

other _____

driver's license number _____

auto insurance company _____

policy number _____